From Rubbish to Riches

Paper

Daniel Nunn

www.raintreepublishers.co.uk
Visit our website to find out more information about Raintree books.

To order:
☎ Phone 0845 6044371
📄 Fax +44 (0) 1865 312263
🖥 Email myorders@raintreepublishers.co.uk

Customers from outside the UK please telephone +44 1865 312262

Raintree is an imprint of Capstone Global Library Limited, a company incorporated in England and Wales having its registered office at 7 Pilgrim Street, London, EC4V 6LB – Registered company number: 6695582

Edited by Rebecca Rissman, Daniel Nunn, and Sian Smith
Designed by Joanna Hinton-Malivoire
Picture research by Tracy Cummins
Originated by Capstone Global Library Ltd
Printed and bound in China by South China Printing Company Ltd

ISBN 978 1 406 22679 9
15 14 13 12 11
10 9 8 7 6 5 4 3 2 1

British Library Cataloguing in Publication Data
Nunn, Daniel. Paper. – (From rubbish to riches)
1. Paper work 2. Waste paper–Recycling 3. Trash art-
4. Refuse and refuse disposal- 5. Salvage
745.5'4-dc22
A full catalogue record for this book is available from the British Library.

Acknowledgements
We would like to thank the following for permission to reproduce photographs: Alamy pp. 9, 23a (Vincent L. Long), 22a (© Carole Hewer); Heinemann Raintree pp. 4 (David Rigg), 5, 6, 10, 11, 12, 13, 14, 15, 16, 17, 18, 19, 20, 21, 23b, 23c (Karon Dubke); Shutterstock pp. 7 (© Picsfive), 8, 23d (© Patty Orly), 22b (© Nattika), 22c (© spaxiax).

Cover photograph of paper sack reproduced with permission of istockphoto (© René Mansi). Cover image of papier mâché reproduced with permission of Shutterstock (Andrew Olscher). Back cover photographs of a table mat and a mask reproduced with permission of Heinemann Raintree (Karon Dubke).

Every effort has been made to contact copyright holders of material reproduced in this book. Any omissions will be rectified in subsequent printings if notice is given to the publisher.

Disclaimer
All the internet addresses (URLs) given in this book were valid at the time of going to press. However, due to the dynamic nature of the internet, some addresses may have changed, or sites may have changed or ceased to exist since publication. While the author and publisher regret any inconvenience this may cause readers, no responsibility for any such changes can be accepted by either the author or the publisher.

Contents

Some words are shown in bold, **like this**. You can find them in the glossary on page 23.

What is paper?

Paper is a **material** we write on.

Paper is made from trees.

Books, magazines, newspapers, and notepads are all made of paper.

Napkins, plates, and cups can all be made of paper, too!

What happens when you throw paper away?

Paper is very useful.

But when you have finished with it, do you throw it away?

If you throw paper away it will end up at a rubbish tip.

It will be buried in the ground and may stay there for a very long time.

What is recycling?

It is much better to **recycle** paper instead of throwing it away.

Separate paper from your other rubbish and then put it in a recycling bin.

The paper will be collected and taken to a **factory**.

Then the paper will be made into something new.

How can I reuse old paper?

You can also use old paper to make your own new things.

When you have finished with something made out of paper, put it to one side instead of throwing it away.

Soon you will have lots of paper waiting to be reused.

You are ready to turn your rubbish into riches!

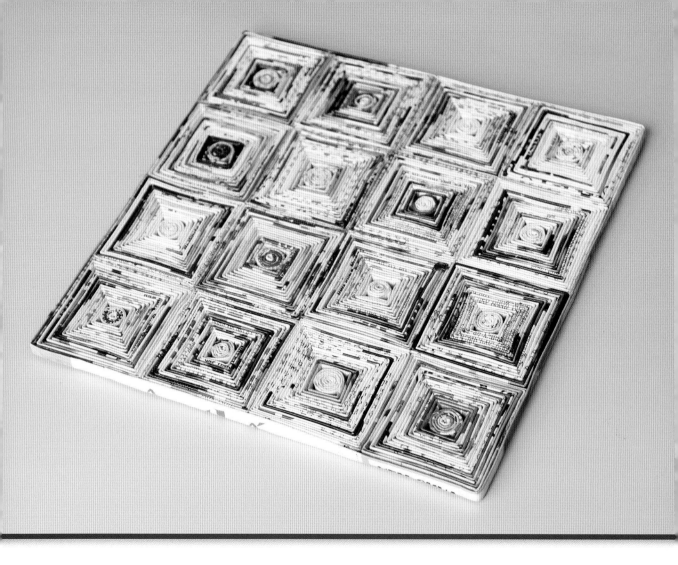

Magazines can be made into colourful table mats.

This table mat has been made by folding up pages from magazines.

You can also cut up paper to make beautiful **mosaics**.

This picture of a bird is made out of lots of tiny pieces of old paper.

What can I make with paper cups and bags?

You can use an old paper cup to make a fun ball-and-cup game.

Try to catch the ball in the cup – it's harder than it looks!

Paper bags make great puppets!

What sort of paper bag puppet will you make?

What else can I make with paper?

You can make all sorts of things with **papier mâché**.

These children are wearing papier mâché masks.

Making papier mâché can be a bit messy.

Why not keep clean by wearing an apron made of old newspapers?

Make your own magazine nameplate

You can use old magazines to make a nameplate for your bedroom door.

You will need a piece of card, scissors, glue, and a pile of old magazines.

First, decide what you want your nameplate to say.

Then cut out the letters that you need from the magazines. Do not use sharp scissors without help from an adult.

Arrange the letters in the right order on the card.

Then carefully glue each letter to the card.

Wait for the glue to dry.

Your nameplate is ready to be fixed to your bedroom door!

Recycling quiz

One of these things is made from **recycled** paper. Can you guess which one? (Answer on page 24.)

Glossary

 factory building where something is made

 material what something is made of

 mosaic picture made from small pieces of paper, glass, or tiles

 papier mâché mixture of shredded paper and glue used to make things. It goes hard when it is dry.

 recycle break down a material and use it again to make something new

Find out more

Ask an adult to help you make fun things with paper using the websites below.

Ball-and-cup game: **www.lakeshorelearning. com/general_content/free_resources/crafts/mt_ catchthebead.jsp**

Fruit and vegetables: **familyfun.go.com/crafts/papier- mache-veggies-661990/**

Table mats**: www.clevernesting.com/2009/07/ recycled-magazine-page-coaster-tutorial/**

Answer to question on page 22
The cat is made from recycled paper.

Index